Launching Your Career

Time Management for Young Professionals

Paul R. DeCoster

Copyright © 2024

All Rights Reserved

ISBN: 9798344228327

About the Author

Paul DeCoster, the author of Field Guide for A Winning Sales Organization: A Practical Guide to Sales Operations, has dedicated his career to empowering sales professionals. With a diverse 15-year tenure, he has witnessed the common challenge of effective time management, which plagues both novices and seasoned experts alike. This realization inspired his latest work, which serves as a comprehensive guide to mastering this critical skill.

Mr. DeCoster understands the importance of time management for young professionals, knowing that it can make the difference between stagnant careers and rapid advancement. Effective time management is the cornerstone of professionalism, enabling individuals to prioritize tasks, meet deadlines, and optimize their productivity. It is a skill that, when honed across teams, can drive revenue growth and cost optimization, as Paul has consistently observed throughout his career. This book is designed to be an invaluable tool, offering practical strategies and insights. It aims to equip professionals with the ability to manage their time effectively, ultimately enhancing their performance and career prospects.

Through his work with various organizations, from Fortune 100 firms to struggling startups, Mr. DeCoster has witnessed what makes people successful, or unsuccessful, in time management. By sharing his expertise, Paul hopes to empower professionals to take control of their time, make informed decisions, and ultimately shape their career trajectories. It is this practical focus that sets his work apart, providing readers with a powerful tool to navigate the challenges of modern professional life.

Contents

About the Author i
Chapter 1: Understanding Time Management 1
Chapter 2: Setting Clear Goals 9
Chapter 3: Prioritization Techniques 17
Chapter 4: Creating a Productive Environment 25
Chapter 5: Planning Your Day 33
Chapter 6: Managing Multitasking and Focus 41
Chapter 7: Utilizing Tools and Resources 49
Chapter 8: Overcoming Procrastination 57
Chapter 9: Evaluating Your Time Management 65
Chapter 10: Balancing Work and Life 73

Chapter 1:
Understanding Time Management

The Importance of Time Management

Effective time management is a crucial skill for new college graduates entering the workforce. As they transition from the structured environment of academia to the more fluid and often unpredictable nature of professional life, understanding how to manage their time efficiently can significantly impact their success. The ability to prioritize tasks, set realistic deadlines, and allocate time wisely can lead to enhanced productivity and reduced stress levels, ultimately paving the way for career advancement.

One of the key aspects of time management is the art of prioritization. New graduates often find themselves juggling multiple responsibilities, from work assignments to networking opportunities. Learning to identify which tasks are most urgent and important can help them focus their efforts on what truly matters. Techniques such as the Eisenhower Matrix, which categorizes tasks based on urgency and importance, can be particularly beneficial. By distinguishing between what is crucial and what can be deferred or delegated, young professionals can allocate their time more effectively and avoid feeling overwhelmed.

Setting clear goals is another fundamental component of effective time management.

Graduates should establish short-term and long-term career objectives that provide direction and motivation. Using the SMART criteria—Specific, Measurable, Achievable, Relevant, Time-bound—can aid in creating actionable goals. By breaking down larger objectives into smaller, manageable tasks, individuals can track their progress and adjust their strategies as needed. This structured approach not only enhances focus but also fosters a sense of accomplishment as each milestone is achieved.

Moreover, utilizing technology can significantly enhance time management capabilities. There are numerous tools and applications designed to help professionals organize their schedules, set reminders, and track their productivity. Calendar applications, task management software, and time tracking tools can streamline daily activities and provide insights into how time is being spent. Incorporating these technological resources allows new graduates to stay organized and maintain a clear overview of their commitments, which is essential for effective time management.

Finally, it is important for young professionals to recognize the value of self-care in the context of time management. Balancing work responsibilities with personal life is vital for maintaining overall well-being and productivity. Regular breaks, exercise, and time for relaxation can prevent burnout and enhance focus when returning to tasks. By integrating self-care practices into their schedules, new graduates can improve their time management skills while ensuring they remain energized and motivated in their professional pursuits.

Common Time Management Challenges for New Graduates

New graduates often encounter a range of time management challenges as they transition from the structured environment of college to the more flexible and demanding world of work. One of the primary difficulties is the lack of a defined schedule. In college, students typically follow a set timetable with classes, study sessions, and extracurricular activities, which helps to establish a routine. Once they enter the workforce, however, many young professionals find themselves responsible for creating their own schedules, leading to potential procrastination and disorganization.

Another common challenge is the overwhelming number of tasks and responsibilities that come with a new job. Graduates may feel pressured to perform well, meet deadlines, and impress their supervisors, all while juggling personal commitments. This can result in a sense of being inundated with work, making it difficult to prioritize tasks effectively. Without clear strategies for breaking down projects into manageable steps, new professionals may struggle to maintain productivity and avoid burnout.

Additionally, many new graduates experience difficulty in setting boundaries, particularly when it comes to work-life balance. The desire to prove themselves often leads young professionals to overcommit to work-related projects, sacrificing personal time and interests. This imbalance can lead to stress and dissatisfaction, ultimately affecting both their professional performance and personal well-being. Learning to assertively communicate availability and limits is crucial for sustaining long-term career success and personal fulfillment.

Distractions in the workplace also pose a significant obstacle for recent graduates. The modern office environment is often filled with interruptions, such as meetings, social media, and informal conversations. These distractions can detract from focus and productivity, leading to inefficient use of time. Developing strategies to minimize distractions, such as establishing designated work hours or utilizing techniques like the Pomodoro Technique, can help new graduates maintain their concentration and enhance their overall efficiency.

Lastly, the pressure to continuously learn and adapt in a fast-paced work environment can create time management challenges for new graduates. As industries evolve, young professionals must keep up with new skills and knowledge, which can add to their already full schedules. Finding time for professional development amidst daily responsibilities requires careful planning and prioritization. Emphasizing the importance of lifelong learning while integrating it into their time management strategies will empower graduates to grow in their careers without feeling overwhelmed.

The Benefits of Effective Time Management

Effective time management is a crucial skill for new college graduates entering the workforce. As young professionals transition from the structured environment of academia to the often self-directed nature of a career, mastering time management can significantly impact their productivity and overall success. By organizing their tasks and prioritizing responsibilities, graduates can ensure that they meet deadlines, achieve goals, and maintain a healthy work-life balance. This skill not only enhances individual performance but also contributes to a more positive perception among colleagues and supervisors.

One of the primary benefits of effective time management is increased productivity. When professionals allocate their time wisely, they can focus on high-priority tasks that align with their career objectives. This focus minimizes distractions and allows individuals to engage in deep work, which is essential for mastering complex concepts and producing quality outcomes. Utilizing techniques such as the Pomodoro Technique or time blocking can help graduates structure their work periods, leading to greater efficiency and a sense of accomplishment.

Additionally, effective time management fosters better decision-making. When young professionals take the time to plan and prioritize their tasks, they can approach their responsibilities with a clearer mindset. This clarity reduces the likelihood of feeling overwhelmed and enables graduates to make informed choices about how to allocate their time. Moreover, by identifying which tasks require immediate attention and which can be scheduled for later, professionals can avoid the pitfalls of procrastination and ensure that they remain on track with their projects.

Another significant advantage of mastering time management is the enhancement of personal well-being. New graduates often face pressures from work, social life, and personal commitments. By managing their time effectively, they can create a balanced schedule that accommodates both professional responsibilities and personal interests. This balance is crucial for preventing burnout and maintaining motivation. When individuals carve out time for self-care, hobbies, and social interactions, they are more likely to approach their work with renewed energy and enthusiasm.

Lastly, effective time management can lead to improved professional relationships. When young professionals respect deadlines and deliver quality work, they build a reputation for reliability and competence. This reliability fosters trust among colleagues and supervisors, creating a collaborative atmosphere where teamwork can flourish. Furthermore, when individuals demonstrate strong time management skills, they are often considered for greater responsibilities and leadership roles, setting the stage for long-term career advancement. By embracing time management techniques, new college graduates can not only enhance their performance but also lay a foundation for a successful and fulfilling career.

Launching Your Career

PAUL R. DECOSTER

Chapter 2:
Setting Clear Goals

Short-Term vs Long-Term Goals

Short-term and long-term goals are essential concepts in the realm of time management and career planning, particularly for new college graduates entering the workforce. Short-term goals are typically defined as those that can be achieved within a year or less. These goals often focus on immediate tasks and milestones, such as landing a job, completing a project, or developing a specific skill. In contrast, long-term goals are broader and more strategic, often spanning several years or even decades. They encompass aspirations like career advancement, achieving a leadership position, or gaining expertise in a particular field.

Establishing short-term goals provides a clear roadmap for recent graduates. By breaking down larger objectives into manageable tasks, individuals can create a structured approach to their career development. For instance, a graduate might set a short-term goal of applying to a certain number of jobs each week, attending networking events, or completing relevant online courses. These actionable steps not only foster a sense of accomplishment but also help maintain motivation during the often overwhelming transition from college to the professional world.

On the other hand, long-term goals serve as a guiding vision for one's career. These goals require a more reflective approach, as they involve considering personal values, interests, and aspirations. Long-term goals might include aiming for a specific job title, such as becoming a project manager or director, or pursuing further education, such as obtaining a master's degree. By establishing these broader objectives, graduates can ensure that their short-term efforts align with their ultimate career aspirations, creating a cohesive and purposeful path forward.

Balancing short-term and long-term goals is crucial for effective time management. While short-term goals provide immediate direction and a sense of urgency, long-term goals offer a perspective that helps individuals prioritize their daily activities. Graduates should regularly review and adjust their goals as needed, ensuring that they remain relevant and attainable. This balance allows for adaptability in a fast-changing job market while keeping the focus on overarching career ambitions.

Finally, integrating both short-term and long-term goals into a comprehensive time management strategy can enhance productivity and satisfaction in one's career. New college graduates should consider creating a visual representation of their goals, such as a goal chart or a timeline, to track their progress and celebrate achievements along the way. This practice not only reinforces commitment but also provides a visual reminder of how daily efforts contribute to larger aspirations. By effectively managing their time and aligning their goals, graduates can launch their careers with confidence and clarity.

SMART Goals Framework

The SMART Goals Framework is a powerful tool for new college graduates navigating their early careers. This approach helps individuals set clear and achievable objectives, ensuring that their efforts are both focused and productive. The acronym SMART stands for Specific, Measurable, Achievable, Relevant, and Time-bound, each component serving a distinct purpose in the goal-setting process. By applying this framework, graduates can enhance their time management skills and increase their chances of success in the competitive job market.

Specificity is crucial when setting goals. A specific goal clearly defines what you want to achieve, eliminating ambiguity and providing direction. For instance, instead of stating, "I want to find a job," a specific goal would be, "I want to secure a marketing position at a tech company."

This specificity gives you a target to aim for and allows you to tailor your actions accordingly. By knowing exactly what you want, you can allocate your time and resources more efficiently, focusing your efforts on the necessary steps to reach that goal.

Measurability is the second component, which encourages graduates to quantify their goals. Establishing measurable criteria helps track progress and maintain motivation. For example, if your goal is to network effectively, you might set a measurable target of attending three networking events each month and connecting with at least five professionals at each event. This not only provides a way to assess your progress but also enables you to celebrate small victories along the way, reinforcing your commitment to your career development.

Achievability is about setting realistic goals that challenge yet remain attainable. It's essential to consider your current skills, resources, and limitations when formulating your objectives. Goals that are too ambitious can lead to frustration and burnout, while those that are too easy may not stimulate growth. For example, aiming to become a senior manager within a year may not be realistic for most new graduates. Instead, focusing on gaining relevant experience and skills in an entry-level role can set the foundation for future advancement.

Finally, a goal must be relevant and time-bound. Relevance ensures that your goals align with your broader career aspirations and personal values, making them meaningful. Time-bound goals incorporate deadlines, creating urgency and prompting action. For example, rather than saying, "I want to improve my public speaking skills," a more effective approach would be, "I will participate in a public speaking workshop within the next three months and deliver a presentation to my peers afterward." By integrating these elements, the SMART Goals Framework empowers new graduates to take charge of their career paths with clarity and confidence, ultimately enhancing their time management abilities and professional success.

Aligning Goals with Career Aspirations

Aligning goals with career aspirations is a crucial step for new college graduates entering the workforce. It involves understanding not only what you want to achieve professionally but also how to strategically plan your time and resources to reach those goals. This alignment ensures that your daily activities and long-term plans are coherent, creating a roadmap that guides your career development. By identifying and articulating your aspirations, you can prioritize tasks that propel you toward achieving them.

To begin this process, self-reflection is essential. Take the time to assess your interests, strengths, and values. Consider what aspects of your field excite you the most and where you see yourself in the future. This reflection enables you to set SMART goals—Specific, Measurable, Achievable, Relevant, and Time-bound. For instance, if you aspire to become a project manager, you might set a goal to complete a certification course within a year while gaining relevant experience through internships or volunteer opportunities.

Once you have established your goals, the next step is to create a structured plan that incorporates effective time management techniques. Breaking down your larger goals into smaller, actionable steps can make the process less overwhelming. Utilize tools such as calendars, to-do lists, and project management software to organize tasks and deadlines. Allocating specific time blocks for each task not only helps in maintaining focus but also ensures consistent progress toward your aspirations.

In addition, it is vital to remain flexible and open to adjusting your goals as you gain more experience and insight into your chosen field. The job market is dynamic, and new opportunities may arise that could lead you in unexpected directions. Regularly reviewing and revising your goals helps maintain alignment with your evolving career aspirations. This adaptability is key to navigating the early stages of your professional journey and ensuring that your efforts remain relevant and impactful.

Finally, seek mentorship and networking opportunities to support your goal alignment process. Connecting with professionals in your desired field can provide valuable insights and guidance. Mentors can help you refine your goals based on their experiences and offer advice on effective time management practices tailored to your aspirations. Building a network can also open doors to opportunities that align with your career path, making the journey toward your professional goals more efficient and rewarding.

Chapter 3:
Prioritization Techniques

The Eisenhower Matrix

The Eisenhower Matrix, also known as the Urgent-Important Matrix, is a powerful tool for prioritizing tasks effectively. Developed by President Dwight D. Eisenhower, this technique helps individuals distinguish between what is urgent and what is important, allowing for more strategic decision-making. For new college graduates entering the professional world, mastering this matrix can significantly enhance productivity and reduce stress. By categorizing tasks into four quadrants, graduates can allocate their time and energy to the activities that truly matter in their careers.

The first quadrant encompasses tasks that are both urgent and important. These are often crises or deadlines that demand immediate attention. For young professionals, this may include completing a project due soon, addressing urgent issues at work, or responding to critical emails. While it's essential to address tasks in this quadrant promptly, relying solely on this category can lead to burnout and reactive work habits. Graduates should strive to minimize the number of tasks that fall into this quadrant by planning ahead and anticipating challenges.

The second quadrant is where the most significant opportunities for growth and long-term success lie. Tasks that are important but not urgent fall here. These may include planning for future projects, networking, professional development, and setting career goals. By focusing on activities in this quadrant, new graduates can cultivate skills and relationships that will pay dividends over time. Allocating time for these essential tasks can help prevent them from becoming urgent crises later on, enabling a proactive rather than reactive approach to career management.

The third quadrant includes tasks that are urgent but not important. These often involve interruptions or requests from others that may seem pressing but do not contribute significantly to personal or professional goals. For young professionals, this could be responding to non-essential emails or attending meetings that do not require their direct involvement. Graduates should learn to recognize these tasks and consider delegating them or setting boundaries to protect their time, focusing instead on what truly matters for their career advancement.

The fourth quadrant contains tasks that are neither urgent nor important. These activities can often lead to wasted time and should be minimized or eliminated altogether. For recent graduates, this might include excessive social media browsing or engaging in time-consuming but unproductive distractions. By being mindful of activities that fall into this category, young professionals can reclaim valuable time and redirect their efforts toward tasks that align with their career aspirations. Embracing the Eisenhower Matrix can empower new graduates to manage their time more effectively, ensuring they prioritize what truly contributes to their long-term success.

ABCD Prioritization Method

The ABCD Prioritization Method is a powerful tool designed to assist new college graduates in managing their time effectively as they transition into the professional world. This method helps individuals categorize tasks based on their importance and urgency, enabling them to focus on what truly matters. By implementing this technique, young professionals can enhance their productivity and ensure that they are not merely busy but engaged in activities that contribute to their long-term goals.

In the ABCD framework, tasks are classified into four categories: A, B, C, and D. "A" tasks are those that are highly important and urgent, requiring immediate attention. These are the tasks that can significantly impact your career progress, such as meeting deadlines for critical projects or preparing for job interviews. "B" tasks are important but not urgent, meaning they should be scheduled for a later time but still require your focus. Examples include networking with industry professionals or developing new skills that can enhance your employability.

"C" tasks are categorized as less important but urgent, often representing interruptions or requests from others that demand attention but do not contribute significantly to your long-term goals. These might include responding to emails or attending meetings that could be streamlined. Finally, "D" tasks are neither important nor urgent and can often be postponed or eliminated altogether. These might include unnecessary social media browsing or tasks that add little to your professional development.

To effectively use the ABCD Prioritization Method, begin by listing all your current tasks and projects. Once you have your list, assign each task a letter based on its importance and urgency. This exercise not only clarifies what needs your immediate focus but also helps you identify tasks that can be delegated or eliminated. By regularly revisiting and adjusting your priorities, you can maintain a clear focus on your most impactful activities.

Ultimately, the ABCD Prioritization Method empowers new graduates to take control of their time and make informed decisions about where to direct their efforts. By distinguishing between tasks that are truly critical and those that are simply distractions, young professionals can cultivate a more effective workflow. This structured approach to prioritization not only enhances productivity but also contributes to a greater sense of accomplishment and career satisfaction as you navigate the early stages of your professional journey.

The 80/20 Rule (Pareto Principle)

The 80/20 Rule, also known as the Pareto Principle, is a powerful concept that can significantly enhance your time management skills as a new college graduate entering the workforce. This principle suggests that roughly 80% of effects come from 20% of causes. In the context of your career, this means that a small portion of your efforts can yield the majority of your results. By identifying and focusing on these critical tasks, you can maximize your productivity and effectiveness in your new role.

To implement the 80/20 Rule effectively, begin by assessing your daily tasks and responsibilities. Take note of which activities contribute the most to your goals and success in your job. You might find that a handful of key tasks, such as networking with colleagues, completing high-impact projects, or acquiring new skills, drive the majority of your achievements. Prioritizing these tasks over less impactful activities can free up time and energy for what truly matters, allowing you to make more significant strides in your career.

One practical approach to applying the 80/20 Rule is to categorize your tasks based on their importance and urgency. Use a simple matrix to distinguish between tasks that are urgent and important, important but not urgent, urgent but not important, and neither urgent nor important. By concentrating on the tasks that fall into the urgent and important category, you can ensure that you are dedicating your time to activities that will propel your career forward. This method not only helps you manage your time more effectively but also reduces stress by eliminating less critical obligations.

Another critical aspect of the 80/20 Rule is the need for regular reflection and adjustment. As you progress in your career, the tasks that yield the most significant results may change. Set aside time each week or month to evaluate your priorities and determine if your focus is still aligned with your career goals. This habit of reflection will allow you to adapt to new challenges and opportunities, ensuring that you remain productive and on track in your professional journey.

Finally, remember that the 80/20 Rule is not just about individual productivity; it can also be applied to team dynamics and collaboration. As you work with colleagues, identify which team members contribute the most to your collective success and focus on leveraging their strengths. By collaborating with high-impact individuals, you can enhance your own productivity and foster a more efficient work environment. Embracing the Pareto Principle in both personal and professional contexts can lead to a more fulfilling and successful career as a young professional.

PAUL R. DECOSTER

Chapter 4:
Creating a Productive Environment

Organizing Your Workspace

Organizing your workspace is a critical step in enhancing productivity and managing your time effectively as a new college graduate entering the professional world. A well-structured workspace can reduce distractions, streamline processes, and ultimately contribute to a more efficient workday. Start by decluttering your desk; remove any items that do not serve a purpose in your daily tasks. This includes old papers, unnecessary supplies, and personal items that might divert your attention. A clean and organized environment sets the stage for focused work and helps to foster a professional atmosphere.

Once you have cleared your workspace, consider the layout and arrangement of your materials. Place frequently used items within easy reach to minimize disruptions when you need to retrieve them. This may include your computer, notepads, pens, and reference materials. Organizing these tools in a way that makes sense to you can save valuable time during your workday, allowing you to concentrate on your tasks without the frustration of searching for essentials. Utilize drawer organizers or desktop trays to keep your workspace neat and accessible.

In addition to physical organization, digital organization plays a significant role in managing your time effectively. Create a filing system on your computer that mirrors your physical workspace. Use clearly labeled folders to categorize documents, making it easier to locate files when needed. Regularly review and clean up your digital files to avoid unnecessary clutter. Implementing a consistent naming convention for your documents will also facilitate quick access and help you maintain order in your digital workspace.

Establishing a routine for maintaining your organized workspace is essential for long-term success. Set aside a few minutes at the end of each day to tidy up your desk and prioritize tasks for the following day. This practice not only keeps your space orderly but also helps you to mentally prepare for the next day's challenges. By dedicating time to this routine, you will find it easier to start each workday with a clear mind and an organized environment, which can significantly enhance your productivity.

Finally, personalizing your workspace can contribute to both motivation and comfort. While it is important to keep your area professional, adding elements that inspire you or make you feel at ease can improve your overall work experience. Consider incorporating a plant, a motivational quote, or a piece of artwork that resonates with you. Striking the right balance between professionalism and personalization will help you create an environment where you can thrive as you launch your career.

Minimizing Distractions

Minimizing distractions is a crucial skill for new college graduates entering the workforce. In today's fast-paced environment, distractions can stem from various sources, including technology, social media, and even the physical workspace. Recognizing these distractions is the first step in learning to manage them effectively. By understanding how distractions impact productivity, young professionals can take proactive measures to create a more focused work environment.

One of the most significant distractions for young professionals is digital technology. With smartphones and computers constantly buzzing with notifications, it can be challenging to maintain concentration. To combat this, graduates should consider implementing specific techniques like setting their devices to "Do Not Disturb" during work hours. Additionally, using apps designed to block distracting websites can help maintain focus on tasks at hand. Establishing designated times for checking emails and social media can also aid in reducing the urge to divert attention, allowing for deeper engagement in work-related projects.

Another common distraction is the workplace environment itself. Open office layouts, while promoting collaboration, can also lead to excessive noise and interruptions. Graduates can create a distraction-free zone by using noise-cancelling headphones or finding a quieter area to work. Additionally, organizing the workspace can minimize visual distractions. A clean and orderly desk fosters a focused mindset, making it easier to concentrate on tasks without unnecessary clutter competing for attention.

Time management techniques play a vital role in minimizing distractions. The Pomodoro Technique, for instance, encourages young professionals to work in short bursts with scheduled breaks. This approach not only helps maintain focus but also refreshes the mind, making it easier to tackle complex tasks after a brief respite. Setting clear priorities and breaking larger projects into smaller, manageable tasks can also help graduates stay on track and reduce the chances of becoming overwhelmed by distractions.

Finally, self-awareness is essential in the fight against distractions. Young professionals should regularly assess their productivity patterns and identify when they are most susceptible to distractions. Keeping a distraction journal can be an effective way to track when and how often diversions occur. By identifying triggers, graduates can develop strategies to address them, whether through scheduling focused work sessions during peak productivity hours or employing mindfulness techniques to enhance concentration. By actively managing distractions, new graduates can set a strong foundation for a successful career.

The Role of Technology in Time Management

Technology plays a pivotal role in enhancing time management for young professionals, particularly for recent college graduates who are navigating the complexities of their new careers. As these individuals transition from the structured environment of academia to the more fluid demands of the workplace, leveraging technology can significantly improve their ability to prioritize tasks and meet deadlines. Modern tools and applications can help manage schedules, track progress, and facilitate communication, making it easier for graduates to adapt to their new roles.

One of the most significant advancements in time management technology is the availability of digital calendars. Tools like Google Calendar or

Microsoft Outlook allow users to schedule meetings, set reminders, and block time for specific tasks. These platforms often integrate with other applications, enabling seamless task management across different devices. For new graduates, using digital calendars can help them stay organized and ensure they allocate sufficient time for both professional responsibilities and personal commitments. The ability to visualize their schedule in a clear format empowers them to make informed decisions about how to allocate their time effectively.

Task management apps, such as Trello or Asana, provide young professionals with a structured way to organize their projects and daily tasks. These applications allow users to create to-do lists, set deadlines, and track progress on multiple assignments simultaneously. By utilizing these tools, recent graduates can break down larger projects into manageable steps, reducing the feeling of being overwhelmed. Furthermore, many of these platforms offer collaborative features, enabling teams to work together more efficiently. This collaborative capability is particularly valuable in a professional environment where teamwork is often essential to success.

Communication technologies also play a crucial role in time management by streamlining interactions among colleagues. Instant messaging platforms like Slack or Microsoft Teams facilitate quick exchanges of information, reducing the time spent on email correspondence. These tools allow young professionals to stay connected with their team members, ask questions in real-time, and share updates on projects without formal meetings. Effective communication helps prevent misunderstandings and keeps projects moving forward, ultimately leading to better time management and productivity.

Lastly, the rise of automation tools offers young professionals the opportunity to save time on repetitive tasks. Applications like Zapier or IFTTT enable users to create automated workflows that link various apps and services. For instance, they can automatically save email attachments to cloud storage or post updates to social media at scheduled times. By automating routine tasks, recent graduates can focus their energy on more strategic aspects of their work, enhancing their overall productivity. Embracing these technologies not only helps in managing time more effectively but also positions young professionals to adapt to the ever-evolving demands of the workplace.

Chapter 5:
Planning Your Day

Daily Scheduling Techniques

Daily scheduling techniques are essential tools for new college graduates transitioning into the professional world. Establishing a structured daily routine can significantly enhance productivity and reduce the stress associated with managing multiple responsibilities. By adopting effective scheduling methods, young professionals can prioritize tasks, allocate time efficiently, and create a balance between work and personal life. Here are some key techniques to consider when crafting your daily schedule.

One of the most effective methods for daily scheduling is the use of time blocking. This technique involves allocating specific blocks of time for different tasks throughout the day. By setting aside dedicated time for each task, graduates can minimize distractions and increase focus. For example, a young professional might designate the morning hours for deep work, such as project development or important meetings, while reserving the afternoon for administrative tasks and emails. Time blocking not only helps in organizing the day but also encourages accountability, as individuals are more likely to stay on track when they know exactly what they should be working on at any given moment.

Another useful technique is the prioritization of tasks using the Eisenhower Matrix. This method categorizes tasks based on their urgency and importance, helping graduates to identify what needs immediate attention versus what can be scheduled for later. By placing tasks into four quadrants—urgent and important, important but not urgent, urgent but not important, and neither urgent nor important—young professionals can streamline their focus. This approach fosters an understanding of where to invest time and energy, ultimately leading to more efficient decision-making and improved time management.

Incorporating technology can also enhance daily scheduling. Numerous apps and tools are designed to assist in managing time effectively. Calendar applications like Google Calendar or project management tools like Trello and Asana can help graduates visualize their schedules and deadlines. Setting reminders and alerts within these applications ensures that important tasks are not overlooked. Additionally, leveraging technology allows for easy adjustments, enabling young professionals to adapt their schedules as new priorities emerge throughout the day.

Finally, establishing a consistent review process at the end of each day can significantly improve future scheduling. Taking time to reflect on what was accomplished, what challenges were faced, and what adjustments are needed for the next day helps to cultivate a proactive approach to time management. This routine not only aids in recognizing patterns in productivity but also encourages a mindset of continuous improvement. By regularly assessing and refining their daily schedules, young professionals can enhance their effectiveness and better navigate the complexities of the workplace.

Time Blocking Method

The Time Blocking Method is a powerful time management technique that can significantly enhance productivity for new college graduates entering the workforce. This method involves dividing your day into distinct blocks of time, each dedicated to specific tasks or activities. By allocating set periods for various responsibilities, you create a structured schedule that minimizes distractions and encourages focused work. This technique not only helps in managing work tasks effectively but also in balancing personal commitments, allowing for a well-rounded approach to daily life.

To implement the Time Blocking Method, start by identifying your priorities and breaking them down into manageable tasks. List out your responsibilities, both professional and personal, and estimate how much time each task will require. This clarity helps in creating a realistic schedule. Once you have your tasks organized, assign them to specific time blocks throughout your day. For instance, you might reserve the first two hours of the morning for deep work, like project development, followed by a block for meetings and emails. By defining these periods, you establish a clear roadmap for your day, reducing the likelihood of procrastination.

One of the key benefits of time blocking is its ability to foster deep work. With distractions minimized, you are more likely to enter a state of flow, where you can concentrate fully on a single task without interruption. This is particularly important for recent graduates who may be transitioning into roles that require intense focus and creativity. By dedicating uninterrupted time to significant tasks, you can improve your output quality and efficiency, ultimately leading to a more successful professional life.

Moreover, the Time Blocking Method encourages accountability. When you have a set schedule, it becomes easier to track your progress and hold yourself responsible for completing tasks within the designated time frames. This accountability not only enhances your productivity but also builds a sense of accomplishment as you check off completed tasks. For young professionals, developing this habit early on can lead to a greater sense of control over their work and a stronger foundation for future career growth.

Lastly, flexibility is a crucial aspect of the Time Blocking Method. While it's essential to stick to your schedule, unexpected events may arise that require adjustments. Embrace the need to adapt your time blocks as necessary, and don't hesitate to reallocate time for urgent tasks or personal needs. This adaptability ensures that you stay productive without feeling overwhelmed, allowing you to maintain a healthy work-life balance. By mastering the Time Blocking Method, new graduates can effectively manage their time, leading to a more organized and fulfilling professional journey.

The Importance of Breaks and Downtime

The significance of breaks and downtime in a young professional's routine cannot be overstated, especially for new college graduates transitioning into the workforce. This demographic often faces the pressure to prove themselves, leading to extended work hours and a relentless focus on productivity. However, research consistently demonstrates that regular breaks are essential for maintaining high levels of performance and avoiding burnout. By incorporating downtime into their schedules, young professionals can enhance their creativity, improve their problem-solving abilities, and sustain their motivation over the long term.

One of the primary benefits of taking breaks is the impact on cognitive function. Continuous work can lead to mental fatigue, diminishing the brain's ability to process information and make decisions. Short, frequent breaks allow the mind to rest and recharge, facilitating clearer thinking and greater focus when returning to tasks. Techniques such as the Pomodoro Technique, which encourages working in focused bursts followed by brief breaks, can help young professionals manage their time effectively while ensuring their minds remain sharp and engaged.

In addition to cognitive benefits, downtime plays a crucial role in emotional well-being. The transition from college to a professional environment can be overwhelming, and the pressure to excel can lead to increased stress and anxiety. Incorporating breaks into a daily routine provides an opportunity for individuals to step back, reflect, and engage in self-care activities, whether it be going for a walk, practicing mindfulness, or simply enjoying a moment of solitude. These practices can foster resilience, allowing young professionals to better cope with workplace challenges.

Moreover, breaks can enhance creativity and innovation. When individuals are constantly immersed in work, their ability to think outside the box can become stifled. Taking time away from tasks opens the mind to new ideas and perspectives. Engaging in leisure activities, hobbies, or even socializing with peers during downtime can stimulate creativity, providing fresh insights that can be applied to work-related challenges. This creative regeneration is vital for careers that demand innovative thinking and problem-solving.

Finally, the importance of breaks and downtime extends beyond personal productivity; it also influences workplace culture. Young professionals who model healthy work-life balance by taking breaks encourage their colleagues to do the same. This can lead to a more supportive and collaborative environment, where employees feel valued for their well-being as well as their output. By prioritizing breaks, new graduates can contribute to a workplace that recognizes the importance of mental health and productivity, ultimately fostering a more sustainable and enjoyable work experience for all.

Chapter 6:
Managing Multitasking and Focus

The Myth of Multitasking

The concept of multitasking has long been heralded as a desirable skill in the modern workplace, especially for new college graduates entering a fast-paced environment. However, research increasingly indicates that multitasking is more myth than reality. The human brain is not designed to handle multiple tasks simultaneously. Instead, what we perceive as multitasking is often rapid task-switching, which can lead to decreased efficiency and increased errors. Understanding this distinction is crucial for young professionals looking to optimize their time management strategies.

When individuals attempt to juggle multiple tasks at once, they often sacrifice quality for quantity. Studies have shown that performance can significantly drop when people switch between tasks frequently. This decline is attributed to the cognitive load associated with shifting focus from one activity to another, which can take time and mental energy. For new graduates, who may already be navigating the challenges of a new job, recognizing the limitations of multitasking can help streamline their efforts and enhance productivity.

Moreover, the myth of multitasking can foster an unhealthy work culture that glorifies busyness over effectiveness. Young professionals may feel pressured to appear constantly engaged, leading them to adopt multitasking behaviors that ultimately hinder their performance. This culture can result in burnout and decreased job satisfaction, which are detrimental to both personal well-being and career advancement. By challenging the notion that multitasking is a valuable skill, new graduates can prioritize their tasks more effectively and maintain a healthier work-life balance.

To combat the pitfalls of multitasking, young professionals can employ time management techniques that emphasize focus and single-tasking. Strategies such as the Pomodoro Technique, where work is broken into intervals with short breaks, can enhance concentration and improve overall productivity. Additionally, prioritizing tasks using methods such as the Eisenhower Matrix can help graduates identify what is urgent and important, allowing them to allocate their time and energy more wisely.

In conclusion, the myth of multitasking can be detrimental to the careers of new college graduates. By understanding the limitations of their cognitive capabilities and adopting focused time management techniques, young professionals can enhance their productivity and overall job performance.

Embracing single-tasking not only leads to better work outcomes but also fosters a healthier approach to professional responsibilities, setting the stage for long-term career success.

Strategies for Maintaining Focus

Maintaining focus in a fast-paced work environment is crucial for new college graduates who are transitioning into their professional careers. One effective strategy is setting clear, achievable goals. By breaking larger tasks into smaller, manageable objectives, young professionals can create a sense of direction and accomplishment. This approach not only enhances motivation but also helps in prioritizing tasks based on urgency and importance. Utilizing tools such as SMART goals—Specific, Measurable, Achievable, Relevant, and Time-bound—can provide clarity and structure, ensuring that focus remains on what truly matters.

Another vital strategy for maintaining focus is managing distractions effectively. In today's digital age, distractions abound, from social media notifications to chatty coworkers. To combat this, young professionals should consider implementing techniques such as the Pomodoro Technique, which involves working in focused bursts followed by short breaks. This method not only aids concentration but also allows for regular intervals of rest, preventing burnout. Additionally, creating a dedicated workspace free from distractions can significantly enhance productivity and focus during work hours.

Time blocking is another powerful technique that can help maintain focus throughout the day. By allocating specific blocks of time to particular tasks or projects, graduates can ensure that they dedicate their full attention to one thing at a time. This strategy minimizes the tendency to multitask, which can dilute focus and lead to decreased efficiency. It is crucial to assess and adjust these time blocks based on personal productivity patterns, ensuring alignment with when one is most alert and capable of deep work.

Incorporating regular reviews and reflections into one's routine can also support sustained focus. Taking time at the end of each week to evaluate accomplishments, setbacks, and areas for improvement helps in reinforcing positive habits and strategies. This practice not only fosters a growth mindset but also enables young professionals to recalibrate their focus for the following week. Such reflective practices can illuminate patterns in productivity and focus, guiding individuals to make informed adjustments to their time management techniques.

Lastly, fostering a healthy work-life balance is essential for maintaining sustained focus. New graduates should prioritize self-care, including regular physical activity, adequate sleep, and social interactions. These elements contribute to mental clarity and emotional resilience, which are crucial for maintaining focus in professional settings. Additionally, establishing boundaries between work and personal life can prevent burnout and keep motivation levels high. By being mindful of their overall well-being, young professionals can create an environment conducive to sustained focus and productivity.

Techniques for Task Switching

Task switching is a common necessity in today's fast-paced work environment, particularly for new college graduates who often juggle multiple responsibilities. Understanding effective techniques for task switching can enhance productivity and reduce the cognitive load that comes with frequently shifting focus. By mastering these techniques, young professionals can navigate their daily tasks more efficiently and make better use of their time.

One effective technique for task switching is the Pomodoro Technique, which involves breaking work into intervals, traditionally 25 minutes in length, separated by short breaks. This method helps maintain focus and reduces the mental fatigue associated with lengthy, uninterrupted work periods. After completing a Pomodoro, taking a five-minute break allows your mind to reset before tackling the next task. This structured approach not only enhances concentration but also creates a rhythm that can make switching tasks feel more manageable.

Another valuable strategy is prioritization, which involves assessing the urgency and importance of tasks before switching focus. Using a priority matrix can help young professionals categorize tasks into four quadrants: urgent and important, important but not urgent, urgent but not important, and neither. By clearly identifying which tasks require immediate attention, graduates can allocate their time and energy more effectively, ensuring that they switch to tasks that align with their goals and deadlines.

Establishing boundaries is also critical when it comes to task switching. Young professionals should designate specific times during the day for focused work and minimize distractions during these periods. This may include silencing notifications, closing unnecessary browser tabs, or using apps that block social media. By creating an environment conducive to focus, graduates can transition more smoothly between tasks without the temptation to engage in distractions that can derail their productivity.

Lastly, reflection and adjustment are essential components of successful task switching. After completing a series of tasks, taking the time to review what worked well and what didn't can provide valuable insights. Young professionals should ask themselves questions like whether their task-switching techniques were effective, if they felt overwhelmed, or if they were able to maintain their focus. This practice of reflection enables continuous improvement and helps graduates refine their approach to managing time and tasks in a way that best suits their individual working styles.

Chapter 7:
Utilizing Tools and Resources

Digital Tools for Time Management

In today's fast-paced professional environment, digital tools have become essential for effective time management. For new college graduates stepping into their careers, leveraging technology can significantly enhance productivity and organization. Various applications and platforms are available to help manage tasks, schedules, and projects, enabling young professionals to navigate their new responsibilities with greater ease and efficiency.

One of the most popular categories of digital tools for time management is task management applications. Tools like Todoist, Trello, and Asana allow users to create to-do lists, set deadlines, and prioritize tasks. These platforms offer features such as reminders and progress tracking, which can help graduates stay on top of their responsibilities. By breaking down larger projects into manageable tasks, young professionals can avoid feeling overwhelmed and maintain a clear focus on their goals.

Calendar applications are another critical component of effective time management. Platforms like Google Calendar and Microsoft Outlook provide a centralized place to schedule meetings, deadlines, and personal commitments.

By utilizing shared calendars, young professionals can coordinate with colleagues and avoid scheduling conflicts. These applications often come with features that allow for color-coding events, setting recurring appointments, and sending notifications, fostering better organization and time allocation.

Time tracking tools are beneficial for those who want to gain insight into how they spend their time. Applications such as Toggl and Clockify enable users to monitor their activities throughout the day, helping them identify patterns and areas for improvement. By analyzing time spent on various tasks, new graduates can make informed adjustments to their schedules, ensuring they allocate sufficient time to priority projects while minimizing distractions and time-wasting activities.

Lastly, integrating productivity techniques with digital tools can lead to even greater efficiency. Methods such as the Pomodoro Technique can be enhanced with apps that provide timers and tracking capabilities. By using technology to implement these strategies, graduates can foster a disciplined work routine that encourages focus and breaks, ultimately leading to improved output and job satisfaction. Embracing digital tools for time management not only supports young professionals in their current roles but also equips them with skills that will benefit their careers in the long run.

Apps for Task Management

In today's fast-paced work environment, effective task management is crucial for young professionals striving to make their mark. With the myriad of responsibilities that come with starting a new career, using apps designed for task management can significantly enhance productivity and organization. These digital tools help streamline workflows, prioritize tasks, and ensure that critical deadlines are met, allowing new graduates to focus on delivering high-quality work.

One of the most popular types of task management apps is the to-do list application. Apps like Todoist and Microsoft To Do allow users to create simple yet effective lists that can be categorized by project, due date, or priority level. The ability to break down larger projects into smaller, manageable tasks helps prevent overwhelm and provides a clear path to completion. Additionally, many of these apps offer features such as reminders and notifications, which serve as helpful prompts to keep users on track.

Another essential category of task management apps includes project management tools, such as Trello and Asana. These platforms are designed for collaboration and offer a visual way to manage tasks and projects. Users can create boards or timelines that outline the various stages of a project, assign responsibilities to team members, and track progress in real time. For new graduates working in team settings, these tools facilitate communication and ensure that everyone is aligned on project goals, ultimately leading to increased efficiency and productivity.

Time tracking apps can also be invaluable for young professionals who are keen on honing their time management skills. Applications such as Toggl and Clockify allow users to track how much time they spend on various tasks and projects throughout the day. By analyzing this data, new graduates can identify patterns in their work habits, recognizing areas where they might be wasting time or could improve efficiency. This insight is crucial for refining their approach to work and ensuring that they allocate time wisely across different responsibilities.

Lastly, many task management apps offer integration with other tools and platforms, creating a seamless workflow for users. For instance, integrating calendar apps like Google Calendar with task management tools can help ensure that deadlines are not only met but are also scheduled into daily routines. This level of organization reduces the risk of missing important tasks and allows new graduates to maintain a clearer overview of their responsibilities, ultimately leading to greater success in their early careers. By leveraging these powerful tools, young professionals can establish effective time management habits that will serve them well throughout their professional journeys.

The Role of Calendars and Planners

Calendars and planners serve as essential tools for new college graduates entering the workforce. They help in organizing schedules, setting priorities, and managing time effectively. Understanding how to leverage these tools can significantly enhance productivity and reduce the stress that often accompanies the transition from academia to a professional environment. By integrating calendars and planners into daily routines, young professionals can ensure they stay on top of deadlines, appointments, and personal commitments.

Digital calendars, such as Google Calendar or Outlook, offer features that allow graduates to synchronize their schedules across multiple devices. This accessibility ensures that important dates and meetings are always at their fingertips. Color-coding events and setting reminders can also help in distinguishing between work-related and personal tasks. By utilizing these features, young professionals can create a clear visual representation of their time commitments, making it easier to allocate time effectively and avoid scheduling conflicts.

Traditional planners, whether paper-based or digital, provide a tangible way to jot down thoughts, track goals, and reflect on progress. Many graduates find that writing tasks by hand helps reinforce memory and commitment to those tasks. A planner can serve as a personal accountability partner, where individuals can review their achievements and adjust their strategies as needed. This reflective practice is vital for continual improvement and can foster a sense of accomplishment as one checks off completed tasks.

In addition to daily and weekly planning, both calendars and planners can be instrumental in long-term goal setting. Graduates should take the time to map out their career objectives and major milestones they want to achieve within specific timeframes. By breaking down larger goals into manageable tasks and scheduling them into their calendars or planners, young professionals can maintain focus and motivation over time. This structured approach not only helps in tracking progress but also instills a sense of purpose in daily activities.

Finally, the consistency of using calendars and planners can lead to the development of positive habits that enhance overall time management skills. By dedicating a few moments each day to review and plan, graduates can establish routines that promote better organization and efficiency. Over time, these habits contribute to a more balanced life, allowing young professionals to thrive in their careers while still making time for personal interests and relationships. Emphasizing the importance of these tools in their daily lives will empower graduates to take charge of their time management strategies, paving the way for successful careers.

Chapter 8:
Overcoming Procrastination

Understanding Procrastination

Procrastination is a common challenge faced by many new college graduates as they transition into the professional world. It is the act of delaying or postponing tasks, often leading to increased stress and reduced productivity. Understanding procrastination is crucial for young professionals who wish to manage their time effectively and achieve their career goals. Recognizing the underlying causes of procrastination can help individuals develop strategies to combat it and maintain momentum in their professional lives.

One primary reason for procrastination is fear of failure. Many new graduates place high expectations on themselves, often resulting in anxiety about their performance. This fear can be paralyzing, causing individuals to avoid starting tasks altogether. Additionally, perfectionism can exacerbate this fear, as graduates may feel that they must complete a task flawlessly before they can even begin. Acknowledging these fears and accepting that mistakes are part of the learning process can help mitigate their impact and encourage a more proactive approach to work.

Another significant factor contributing to procrastination is poor time management. New professionals often struggle with prioritizing tasks and estimating how long activities will take. This lack of organization can lead to a feeling of being overwhelmed, prompting individuals to push tasks aside in favor of less demanding activities. Developing strong time management skills, such as setting specific goals, breaking tasks into manageable steps, and using tools like calendars or to-do lists, can greatly enhance productivity and reduce the likelihood of procrastination.

Distractions also play a crucial role in procrastination. In today's digital age, young professionals are constantly bombarded with notifications from social media, emails, and other forms of communication. These distractions can easily divert attention from important tasks, leading to a cycle of avoidance and procrastination. Creating a conducive work environment by minimizing distractions—such as silencing notifications or establishing designated work hours—can help graduates maintain focus and complete their tasks more efficiently.

Finally, understanding the emotional aspects of procrastination is essential. Many individuals procrastinate as a coping mechanism for stress or boredom associated with certain tasks. This behavior can create a negative feedback loop, where the anxiety of unfinished work leads to further avoidance. Developing a positive mindset towards tasks, seeking support from peers or mentors, and incorporating rewards for completing tasks can help break this cycle. By addressing the emotional triggers of procrastination, new graduates can cultivate healthier work habits and enhance their overall productivity in their careers.

Strategies to Combat Procrastination

Procrastination is a common challenge that many new college graduates face as they transition into the professional world. Understanding its root causes is essential for developing effective strategies to combat it. Often, procrastination stems from fear of failure, feeling overwhelmed by tasks, or a lack of motivation. By recognizing these underlying issues, graduates can better prepare themselves to tackle their responsibilities and establish productive habits that will serve them throughout their careers.

One of the most effective strategies to combat procrastination is breaking tasks into smaller, manageable parts. Large projects can appear daunting, leading to avoidance behaviors. By dividing these tasks into smaller, achievable steps, graduates can focus on completing one segment at a time. This not only makes the work feel less overwhelming but also provides a sense of accomplishment as each small task is completed. Setting specific deadlines for these smaller tasks can further enhance productivity and create a structured timeline for achieving larger goals.

Another useful technique is the Pomodoro Technique, which encourages focused work sessions followed by short breaks. This method involves working for a set period, typically 25 minutes, and then taking a 5-minute break. After four cycles, a longer break of 15-30 minutes can be taken. This approach helps maintain concentration and reduces mental fatigue, making it easier to stay engaged with the work. For new graduates who may struggle with maintaining focus, this structured method can significantly enhance productivity and reduce the tendency to procrastinate.

Establishing a dedicated workspace is also crucial in minimizing distractions and fostering a productive environment. When young professionals create a space that is specifically designated for work, they signal to their brains that it is time to focus. This separation from leisure areas can help reinforce a professional mindset. Additionally, minimizing digital distractions by turning off notifications and setting boundaries with social media usage can aid in maintaining concentration on tasks at hand.

Lastly, accountability can play a pivotal role in overcoming procrastination. Sharing goals with a mentor, colleague, or accountability partner can create a sense of obligation to follow through on commitments. Regular check-ins can serve as motivation and provide an opportunity to discuss challenges and progress. Many young professionals find that having someone to report to helps them stay on track and committed to their deadlines, ultimately leading to improved time management and productivity. By implementing these strategies, new graduates can effectively combat procrastination and lay a strong foundation for their careers.

Building Motivation and Accountability

Building motivation and accountability is crucial for new college graduates as they transition into the professional world. Motivation serves as the driving force that propels individuals toward their goals, while accountability ensures that they stay on track and take responsibility for their actions. Together, these elements create a framework that supports effective time management, enabling young professionals to prioritize tasks and achieve their career aspirations.

To cultivate motivation, it is essential to set clear, achievable goals. Young professionals should start by identifying their short-term and long-term objectives, breaking them down into manageable steps. This process not only provides a sense of direction but also helps individuals maintain focus amidst the distractions of a new work environment. By creating a vision board or a written list of goals, graduates can visualize their aspirations, which reinforces their commitment and ignites their passion for achievement.

Accountability can be enhanced through various strategies, including establishing support networks and partnerships. New graduates can benefit from engaging with mentors, colleagues, or accountability groups that share similar career ambitions. Regular check-ins with these individuals can help track progress, discuss challenges, and celebrate milestones. This collaborative approach fosters a sense of responsibility, encouraging young professionals to remain diligent in their efforts while also providing a platform for shared learning and growth.

Incorporating time management tools into daily routines significantly supports motivation and accountability. Tools such as calendars, to-do lists, and project management apps can help graduates organize their tasks and deadlines efficiently. By leveraging technology, young professionals can track their progress in real time, making it easier to identify areas for improvement and adjust their strategies as needed. This structured approach not only enhances productivity but also reinforces a sense of accomplishment as tasks are completed.

Lastly, self-reflection plays a vital role in maintaining motivation and accountability. New graduates should regularly assess their performance, analyzing what strategies work best and where adjustments may be necessary. Journaling or using self-assessment tools can facilitate this reflection process, helping individuals understand their strengths and weaknesses. By recognizing patterns in their behavior and productivity, young professionals can make informed decisions that align with their goals, ultimately fostering a continuous cycle of motivation and accountability in their careers.

Chapter 9:
Evaluating Your Time Management

Reflecting on Your Time Management Practices

Reflecting on your time management practices is crucial for new college graduates as they transition into the professional world. The habits you cultivate during this period will significantly influence your productivity and overall success. Evaluating how you currently manage your time allows you to identify strengths and weaknesses, providing a clearer picture of areas for improvement. This self-assessment is not just about recognizing what works but also about understanding how your unique circumstances and responsibilities shape your time management style.

Start by analyzing your daily routines and identifying where most of your time is spent. This could include work-related tasks, personal projects, or even leisure activities. Keeping a time log for a week can be particularly revealing. Record how much time you allocate to each task and reflect on the effectiveness of your efforts. Are there activities that consume more time than they should? Are you prioritizing tasks that align with your career goals? This exercise helps in understanding the balance between productivity and procrastination, allowing you to make informed adjustments to your schedule.

Next, consider the tools and techniques you currently employ for managing your time. Are you using a planner, digital calendar, or task management app? Evaluate the effectiveness of these tools in helping you stay organized and motivated. Sometimes, the tools themselves can become a source of distraction if they are not utilized effectively. Explore new methods or technology that might enhance your productivity. For instance, techniques like time blocking or the Pomodoro Technique could offer structure to your day and help you maintain focus on important tasks.

In addition, reflect on your work-life balance. As a new professional, it can be tempting to overcommit to work responsibilities at the expense of personal time. This imbalance can lead to burnout and decreased productivity in the long run. Assess how well you are managing your work commitments alongside personal interests and relationships. Establishing boundaries and prioritizing self-care can lead to more effective time management. Remember that downtime is not wasted time; it is essential for rejuvenation and sustained productivity.

Finally, set specific goals for your time management practices moving forward. Based on your reflections, create actionable steps to improve your efficiency. This could involve setting deadlines for projects, learning to delegate tasks, or blocking out time for professional development. By establishing clear goals, you will be able to measure your progress and adjust your strategies as needed. Regularly revisiting your time management practices ensures that you remain agile and responsive to the demands of your career, ultimately leading to greater success as you launch your professional journey.

Adapting Techniques to Fit Your Needs

Adapting techniques to fit your needs is essential for young professionals entering the workforce. As a new college graduate, you may find that the time management strategies you learned in school do not directly translate to a professional environment. It's crucial to assess your individual workflow, responsibilities, and preferences to create a personalized approach that maximizes productivity. This process begins with understanding the various time management techniques available and evaluating which ones resonate with your working style.

One effective technique is the Pomodoro Technique, which involves breaking work into intervals, traditionally 25 minutes of focused work followed by a 5-minute break. This method can help maintain concentration and prevent burnout. However, the duration of work intervals can be adjusted to fit your needs. If you find that you can focus for longer periods, consider extending the work sessions to 40 minutes or even an hour. The key is to experiment with different lengths and determine what allows you to work best while still providing adequate breaks for rejuvenation.

Another popular strategy is time blocking, which involves scheduling specific blocks of time for different tasks or activities throughout your day. This method can be particularly beneficial for young professionals juggling multiple responsibilities or projects. When adapting time blocking to your needs, consider how your energy levels fluctuate throughout the day. If you are more productive in the morning, reserve that time for challenging tasks, and use the afternoon for less demanding activities. Tailoring your schedule in this way can enhance efficiency and help ensure that you are working on the right tasks at the right times.

In addition to these techniques, utilizing digital tools can significantly improve your time management efforts. Tools like task management applications or calendar software can offer customizable features that align with your workflow. Take the time to explore various apps, focusing on those that allow you to set priorities, track progress, and receive reminders. By integrating technology into your time management strategies, you can create a system that not only suits your preferences but also helps you stay organized and accountable.

Ultimately, the process of adapting time management techniques to fit your needs is ongoing. As you gain experience in your career, your responsibilities and priorities may change, requiring you to reassess and adjust your approach periodically. Regularly reflecting on your productivity and the effectiveness of your chosen methods will ensure that you remain agile and responsive to the demands of your professional life. Embrace the journey of discovering what works best for you, and remember that flexibility is key to successfully managing your time as a young professional.

Continuous Improvement in Time Management

Continuous improvement in time management is crucial for new college graduates as they transition into the workforce. This phase of life often comes with increased responsibilities and expectations, making effective time management essential for both personal and professional success. By embracing a mindset of continuous improvement, young professionals can refine their time management strategies, ultimately enhancing productivity and reducing stress.

One of the foundational techniques for continuous improvement is the practice of regular self-assessment. Young professionals should take time to evaluate their current time management habits and identify areas for enhancement. This can involve tracking how time is spent throughout the day and analyzing patterns in productivity. By recognizing which activities consume the most time or lead to procrastination, graduates can make informed decisions about where to focus their efforts for improvement.

Incorporating feedback is another vital aspect of continuous improvement. Young professionals are encouraged to seek input from peers, mentors, or supervisors regarding their time management practices. Constructive feedback can provide new perspectives and highlight blind spots that individuals may not recognize on their own. This collaborative approach not only fosters personal growth but also builds a network of support that can be invaluable in navigating the early stages of a career.

Setting clear, achievable goals is essential for maintaining momentum in time management improvement efforts. Graduates should establish specific objectives that are measurable and time-bound, allowing them to track progress over time. By breaking larger goals into smaller, manageable tasks, young professionals can create a roadmap for improvement. This structured approach not only enhances focus but also encourages a sense of accomplishment as each milestone is reached.

Finally, embracing adaptability is key to continuous improvement in time management. As new challenges and responsibilities arise, young professionals must be willing to adjust their strategies and techniques accordingly. This might involve experimenting with different tools, such as digital calendars or project management apps, to find what works best for individual preferences. By remaining open to change and willing to refine their methods, graduates can develop a robust time management system that evolves with their career, ensuring long-term success and satisfaction in their professional lives.

Chapter 10:
Balancing Work and Life

The Importance of Work-Life Balance

Achieving a healthy work-life balance is crucial for new college graduates as they transition into the professional world. This balance refers to the ability to allocate time effectively between work responsibilities and personal life. In a society that often glorifies overworking, young professionals must prioritize their well-being to foster a productive career. By understanding the significance of work-life balance, new graduates can cultivate a sustainable approach to their professional lives that enhances both personal satisfaction and career growth.

One of the primary benefits of maintaining a work-life balance is improved mental health. Young professionals often face stress from job responsibilities, performance expectations, and the challenges of adapting to a new work environment. By ensuring they have time for relaxation, hobbies, and social interactions, graduates can mitigate feelings of burnout and anxiety. Engaging in activities outside of work helps to recharge mental energy, allowing for increased focus and creativity when returning to professional tasks.

Moreover, a balanced lifestyle can lead to greater job satisfaction and productivity. When employees feel fulfilled in their personal lives, they are more likely to bring positivity and motivation into the workplace. This satisfaction can translate into higher levels of engagement and performance, which are essential for career advancement. Employers increasingly recognize the value of work-life balance, often supporting initiatives that promote it, such as flexible working hours or remote options. Young professionals who prioritize balance may find themselves more competitive in the job market as companies seek out individuals who can manage their time effectively.

Work-life balance also strengthens personal relationships, which are vital for emotional support and overall well-being. As young professionals establish their careers, they may inadvertently neglect family and friendships due to work commitments. By prioritizing time for loved ones, graduates foster connections that contribute to a supportive network. These relationships not only provide comfort during stressful periods but also encourage a sense of belonging, which is essential for personal growth and resilience in the face of professional challenges.

Lastly, mastering the art of work-life balance equips new graduates with essential time management skills. Learning to set boundaries, prioritize tasks, and allocate time for various aspects of life is invaluable for long-term success. Graduates who develop these skills early in their careers are better prepared to handle future responsibilities and challenges. Ultimately, by embracing work-life balance, young professionals can create a fulfilling trajectory that supports both their career ambitions and personal happiness, setting the stage for a rewarding and sustainable professional journey.

Setting Boundaries

Setting boundaries is a crucial skill that young professionals must develop as they transition from the structured environment of college to the more fluid demands of the workplace. Establishing clear limits around work hours, personal time, and social obligations helps in achieving a balanced life, which is essential for long-term success and well-being. Without effective boundaries, young professionals may find themselves overwhelmed by work responsibilities, leading to stress and burnout.

One of the first steps in setting boundaries is to define your priorities. Understand what is most important to you, both in your professional and personal life. This includes recognizing your work commitments, social activities, and personal time. By identifying these priorities, you can make informed decisions about how to allocate your time.

For instance, if you value health and fitness, you might decide to block out time each week for exercise, ensuring that it does not get overshadowed by work obligations.

Communication is key when it comes to enforcing boundaries. Once you have established what your limits are, it is important to communicate them clearly to colleagues, supervisors, and friends. For example, if you decide that you will not check work emails after a certain hour, inform your team of this boundary. This not only sets expectations but also helps others respect your time. Being assertive about your boundaries fosters a culture of respect and understanding within your professional environment.

In addition to communicating your boundaries, it is essential to practice self-discipline in maintaining them. Young professionals may encounter pressure to respond to work demands outside of their designated hours or to participate in social activities that do not align with their priorities. It is important to stay committed to your boundaries, even when faced with challenges. This might involve saying no to extra work assignments that infringe on your personal time or avoiding social events that conflict with your need for rest.

Finally, regularly reassess your boundaries to ensure they continue to serve your needs effectively. As you progress in your career and personal life, your priorities may shift. Take time to reflect on what is working and what is not, adjusting your boundaries as necessary. This flexibility will allow you to adapt to changing circumstances while maintaining a healthy balance between your work and personal life, ultimately setting the stage for a successful and fulfilling career.

Strategies for Personal Time Management

Effective personal time management is essential for new college graduates as they transition into the professional world. With the demands of a career, social life, and personal responsibilities, mastering time management techniques can significantly enhance productivity and reduce stress. One foundational strategy is prioritization, which involves distinguishing between urgent and important tasks. Graduates can utilize tools like the Eisenhower Matrix to categorize their tasks, ensuring they focus on what truly matters rather than getting lost in a sea of less critical activities.

Another vital strategy is setting SMART goals— specific, measurable, achievable, relevant, and time-bound. By defining clear objectives, graduates can create a roadmap for their professional journey. This approach not only clarifies what they want to achieve but also enables them to track their progress and make necessary adjustments along the way. Incorporating short-term and long-term goals can help maintain motivation and provide a sense of accomplishment as milestones are reached.

Time blocking is a practical technique that involves scheduling specific blocks of time for different activities throughout the day. By allocating dedicated time slots for work tasks, networking, and personal development, graduates can create a structured routine that minimizes distractions and maximizes focus. This method also encourages the establishment of boundaries, ensuring that personal time is respected and protected from work-related interruptions.

Another effective method is leveraging technology to enhance time management. Various apps and tools can assist in organizing tasks, setting reminders, and tracking progress. For example, project management tools like Trello or Asana can help graduates manage multiple projects simultaneously, while calendar apps can ensure important deadlines and appointments are not overlooked. By embracing these digital solutions, young professionals can streamline their workflow and maintain a clear perspective on their responsibilities.

Finally, reflecting on and adjusting time management strategies is crucial for ongoing improvement. Regularly assessing what works and what doesn't allows graduates to fine-tune their approaches, adapting to changing circumstances and responsibilities. Techniques such as maintaining a journal to track time spent on various activities can provide valuable insights. By fostering a mindset of continuous improvement, new graduates can develop sustainable time management practices that support both their professional growth and personal well-being.

www.ingramcontent.com/pod-product-compliance
Lightning Source LLC
Chambersburg PA
CBHW070350230526
45471CB00006B/2495